WHAT WOULD YOU CHOOSE?

RACE A MONSTER TRUCK OR A SNOWMOBILE?

MEGAMACHINES

HELEN GREATHEAD

Gareth Stevens
PUBLISHING

Please visit our website, www.garethstevens.com.
For a free color catalog of all our high-quality books,
call toll free 1-800-542-2595 or fax 1-877-542-2596.

Cataloging-in-Publication Data

Names: Greathead, Helen.
Title: Megamachines / Helen Greathead.
Description: New York : Gareth Stevens Publishing, 2017. | Series: What would you choose?| Includes index.
Identifiers: ISBN 9781482460797 (pbk.) | ISBN 9781482461749 (library bound) | ISBN 9781482460803 (6 pack)
Subjects: LCSH: Machinery--Juvenile literature.
Classification: LCC TJ147.G724 2017 | DDC 629.04'6--d23

Published in 2017 by Gareth Stevens Publishing
111 East 14th Street, Suite 349
New York, NY 10003

Series editor: Adrian Cole
Art direction: Peter Scoulding
Series designer: D. R. ink
Picture researcher: Diana Morris

Photo credits Action Press/Rex Features: 8b. Aeromobil.com: 1cl, 16b. argot/Fotolia: 19b. Silvan Bachmann/Shutterstock: 5bl. Catarina Belova/Shutterstock: 20br. Bram van der Biezen/AFP/Getty Images: 28cr. BloodhoundSSC.com: 27t. Ben Burchall/Press Association: 14cl. Sergei Butorin/Shutterstock: back cover tl. Brian Cassey/Rex Features: 7t. Jeff Chiu/AP/Press Association: 13t. Tung Chueng/Shutterstock: 16t. Daimler AG: 15c. Dikiiy/Dreamstime: 13b. Dusa Architects: 17t. Elenarts/Shutterstock: back cover br. Environmental Images/Universal Images Group/Rex Features: 25t. Yinan Zhang Gyoginan/Dreamstime: 18c. Imaengine/Dreamstime: 24tr. Image Source/Getty Images: 28bl. Insect World/Shutterstock: 28cl. Marcel Janovic/Shutterstock: front cover r, 9tr. Uli Joos: 24tl. Sergey Kamskylin/Shutterstock: 5t. Zoran Karapancev/Shutterstock: 21cr. PH2 (AC) Mark Kettenhoffen, USN. Wikimedia Commons: 18b. Lamborghini: 5c. Andrew Linnett/MOD: 14b. Local Motors: 17b. Lockheed Corporation. Wikimedia Commons: 26t. Jake Loniak © 2008. Image by kollected: 10t. Marchi Mobile: 1cr, 30tr. Stefan Marjoram/BloodhoundSSC.com: 27b. Maxym /Shutterstock: back cover bl. Konstantinos Morastis/Dreamstime: 30tl. Stan Mott: 7b. NASA: 29b. Natursports/Shutterstock: front cover l, 9tl. Omsignal.com: 24br. Felix Pergande/Dreamstime: 24bl. Planet labs: 29. Rex Features: 23b. Gines Romero/Shutterstock: 6b. Boaz Rottem/Alamy: 8cb. Dan Rowlands/Caters: 8t. Fedor Selivanov/Shutterstock: 8c. Sikorsky.com: 28t. Simasz/Dreamstime: 12br. Skylock: 5br. Softbank Corp.: 30bl. Chris Stanley/Dreamstime: 12cl. Milan Surkala/Dreamstime: 20bl. timquijano/CC Wikimedia Commons: 12bl. Toronto Hippo Tours: 25b. Toyota: 10b, 11b. Alessio Viviani/Dreamstime: 6t. Wessex Water/Julian James/Rex Features: 22t, 22b. CC Wikimedia Commons: 2c, 12c, 30cr. Rob Wilson/ Dreamstime: 21b.

Printed in the United States of America

CPSIA compliance information: Batch CW17GS: For further information contact Gareth Stevens, New York, New York at 1-800-542-2595.

CONTENTS

WOULD YOU CHOOSE

TO SEE THE WORLD ON A PENNY-FARTHING BIKE, GO TO SCHOOL RIDING A HOVERBOARD OR TAKE OFF FOR PARIS IN A FLYING CAR?

***Megamachines* invites you to fasten your seat belt, discover all manner of amazing machines and decide which ones you'd rather try out.**

Read each question,

CONSIDER YOUR OPTIONS,

check out the facts,

see what your friends think (and what we chose) and then make YOUR choice.

RIDE WITH THE COPS IN ITALY ... OR UKRAINE?

WE CHOSE

Italy. In 2003, cash-strapped Ukrainian police used a metal cutout cop car to fool speeding drivers into slowing down. In Italy in 2014, Lamborghini donated one of their Huracán supercars (below) to the Italian police force. It can zoom from 0 to 37 miles per hour (60 km/h) in just 3.2 seconds and hit a top speed of 202 mph (325 km/h)! It features all-wheel-drive, is fitted with a number-plate recognition camera and can flash instant images back to police headquarters.

Didn't you know?
Dubai's police force has a whole fleet of supercars, including a MacLaren MP4-12C, an Aston Martin 177, a Lamborghini Aventador and a Ferrari FF.

SECURE YOUR BIKE WITH A SOLAR-POWERED LOCK ... OR RIDE ALONG A SOLAR BIKE TRACK?

WE CHOSE

The lock. Solar cells in each 330 feet (100 m) of Dutch bike track soak up rays that provide enough electricity to power three homes, but they won't help your bike. The bike lock, however, is intelligent! The Skylock runs on a solar-powered, rechargeable battery. Used with a smartphone, it will unlock at a distance and let you know if anyone's tampering with your bike. Should you have an accident, the lock will automatically message your family.

THE FACTS

THE PENNY-FARTHING BIKE

- was invented in 1871 and got its name because the wheel sizes reminded people of the size difference between a penny coin and a farthing (1/4 penny) coin around at the time
- has one fixed gear and a hard leather saddle
- has solid rubber tires and a cast iron frame
- has a 5-foot (1.5 m) front wheel that was designed for increased speed and a smoother ride

SEE THE WORLD ON A PENNY-FARTHING BIKE ... OR A GO-KART?

THE FACTS

THE GO-KART

- was first raced in a California car park in the 1950s
- became a massive craze in the 1960s
- hasn't changed much since the 1970s, though there are many different makes and sizes
- can reach speeds of up to 62 mph (100 km/h)
- is powered by 2- and 4-stroke engines, or electric motors

WHAT WOULD YOU CHOOSE?

WHAT'S SO SPECIAL ABOUT THE PENNY-FARTHING BIKE?

The penny-farthing bike made cycling history with its high-quality ride and superior speed.

BUT YOU WOULDN'T GO ROUND THE WORLD ON ONE?

Thomas Stevens did, from 1884 to 1887. He traveled 13,522 miles (21,762 km) carrying a pistol and his raincoat, which doubled as a tent. Then, in 2008, Joff Summerfield (above) did it too. He visited four continents, 23 countries and covered 22,000 miles (35,406 km/h), and even crossed the Himalayas and reached Everest base camp!

WHAT'S SO SPECIAL ABOUT KARTING?

Karting isn't just for kids, it's the cheapest form of four-wheeled motorsport there is. Some of the earliest go-karts used lawnmower engines and were sold in kits. Today some Superkarts, with up to 500 cc engines, race at over 140 mph (225 km/h)!

BUT YOU WOULDN'T TAKE ONE AROUND THE WORLD?

Stan Mott did from 1961 to 1964. His kart (and trailer) stood 2 inches (5 cm) off the ground (below). He fitted headlights and a 175 cc Lambretta engine. He covered 38,000 miles (61,155 km) and visited 29 countries. He even drove his go-kart across the Sahara Desert!

AND FINALLY ...

You can fall off the penny-farthing, you can't carry many supplies and it's slow going – 40 miles (64 km) a day on average! You probably won't fall out of the go-kart, but you'll be hard to spot in traffic, you'll have to pay for fuel, and there are lots of parts that might need fixing.

WE CHOSE

Get on the bike. You're less likely to break down, and you'll get a better view!

ARRIVE AT THE SCHOOL PROM IN A MINI COOPER ... OR A ROLLS-ROYCE PHANTOM?

WE CHOSE

The Mini. The Phantom may look beautiful and have a luxurious interior, but we're talking a 22-foot (8.2-m) stretch Mini Cooper that can seat six of you in comfort. You can even get the party started on its dance floor that comes complete with flashing lights, and a surround-sound music system!

TRAVEL HOME BY OUTDOOR ESCALATOR ... OR UNDERGROUND FUNICULAR?

WE CHOSE

The escalator. It takes 8 minutes to travel 1.1 miles (1.8 km) to the top of Israel's Carmelit Funicular, in Haifa, without a view (top left). The escalator in Medellín, Colombia (bottom left), is 2.4 miles (3.85 km) long, as tall as a 28-story building and you can travel to the top in just 6 minutes. Medellín was once the world's murder capital, but the escalator has helped to reduce crime by providing poorer people with an easy way to reach the city center.

RACE A MONSTER TRUCK ... OR A SNOWMOBILE?

Didn't you know?
In 2014, the Raminator broke the world speed record for monster trucks – at 99 mph (159.48 km/h). It took years of careful engineering to create the Raminator, which stands 10 feet (3 m) tall and 12.5 feet (3.8 m) wide.

A monster truck has a lightweight fiberglass body which looks like an ordinary truck or car, combined with the most enormous tires and a massive engine. Most monster trucks are capable of up to 68 miles per hour (110 km/h), but won't go that fast during a circuit race when you leap over ramps and crush cars.

On a snowmobile you're low to the ground, holding handlebars that direct the skis at the front, while a rotating track grips the ice at the back. Snowmobile riders in the Winter X Games perform amazing stunts during the snowmobile freestyle event. They speed up ice ramps and can even do midair flips!

AND FINALLY ...

Both vehicles are dangerous – monster trucks have even killed spectators on more than one occasion, but there are hundreds of snowmobile accidents a year in the US alone.

WE CHOSE

The monster truck. It may not be as fast, but you stand more chance of getting to the end of the race.

THE FACTS

THE EXOSKELETON:

- can change positions from standing to lying virtually flat for maximum speed
- can reach a top speed of 74.5 mph (120 km/h)
- runs on high-energy-density batteries with zero carbon emissions
- is lightweight, but stable thanks to its sturdy backbone

RIDE A THREE-WHEELED EXOSKELETON … OR IN A THREE-WHEEL CAR?

THE FACTS

THE iROAD:

- has one wheel at the back and two 2-kilowatt electric motors
- can cover up to 30 miles (48 km) on one charge
- has a top speed of 37 mph (59.5 km/h)
- is only 33.5 inches (85 cm) wide, but seats two people (front and back)

Didn't you know?
The iRoad is so small that four of them will fit in one normal-sized parking space!

WHAT WOULD YOU CHOOSE?

TELL ME ABOUT THE EXOSKELETON

It was designed by Pasadena Arts Center Student, Jake Loniak, as a completely different way of traveling. Thirty-six pneumatic muscles control the legs, arms and backbone of the vehicle and protect the rider.

WHAT'S IT LIKE TO RIDE?

Actually, you don't ride this machine so much as *wear* it – even the helmet is built in! The frame supports your body, but your body controls the machine. You'll shift positions depending on where you're driving, but at top speed you'll feel like you're flying just above the road surface.

TELL ME ABOUT THE iROAD

It's designed to look like a motorbike, but with the comfort and protection of a car (so no helmet needed). The three wheels make it more stable than a bike, but it's only designed for short journeys, so it won't go far before it needs a recharge.

WHAT'S THE iROAD LIKE TO DRIVE?

Inside feels more like a cockpit than a normal car; the controls are simple to use and once you're rolling it even feels like you're gliding. The iRoad is easy to maneuver, with the back wheel swiveling to steer. It's even designed so you can't tip it over.

AND FINALLY ...

The Exoskeleton hasn't actually been built yet; it needs to pass a lot of tests before it can be used on the road. The iRoad is tried, tested, and launched in 2015.

WE CHOSE

The iRoad. It's so like a motorbike it even leans into corners!

RIDE THE WORLD'S STEEPEST STEEL ROLLER COASTER ... OR THE WORLD'S FASTEST?

WE CHOSE

The fastest. The steepest roller coaster has views of Mount Fuji, Japan. You will free-fall a stomach-flipping 141 feet (43 m) at 121 degrees, reaching speeds of up to 62 mph (100 km/h) (below). However, the fastest roller coaster at Ferrari World, in Dubai (left), travels at a top speed of 149 mph (240 km/h)! You'll need safety goggles as you swish around the tracks in a Formula One Ferrari-style car.

KEEP A FLYING PIGEON ... OR A WASP IN YOUR HOME?

WE CHOSE

The Vespa (it's Italian for wasp) because it's got more vroom! With just one gear and a sturdy black frame, the Flying Pigeon is the most popular bicycle EVER. Owning one in China in the 1950s was a sign of prosperity. The Vespa motor scooter was first produced in Italy in 1946. With its neat design, which protected the engine and its rider, Vespas were soon popular all over the world.

Didn't you know?
Over 75 million Flying Pigeons have been produced since 1950.

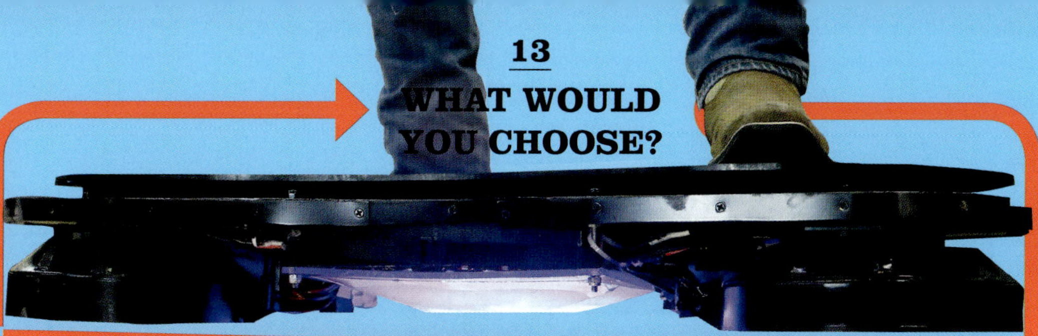

GO TO SCHOOL ON A MOTORIZED SKATEBOARD ... OR A HOVERBOARD?

The idea for the Hoverboard – a floating skateboard – came from the 1989 movie *Back to the Future: Part II*. In 2014 "hovering" was finally made possible through electromagnetic technology. The "Hendo" hoverboard can carry two people, floating 1.2 inches (3 cm) above the ground, for around 15 minutes.

The motorized skateboard has two motors hidden under the board to turn the back wheels. A handheld control lets you move forward, slow down and stop. You can't do tricks on these boards, but you'll coast uphill and ride for up to 6.2 miles (10 km) at a maximum speed of 20 miles per hour (32 km/h).

AND FINALLY ...

Even if your journey to school takes under 15 minutes, it's unlikely you'd get there on a Hoverboard. Because of its electromagnetic technology, it only works on certain metal surfaces. The skateboard doesn't come cheap, but it should get you to school with no trouble.

WE CHOSE

The skateboard. If the battery runs out, you can always move it with your foot!

REMOTE-CONTROLLED TANK ... OR DRIVERLESS TRUCK?

THE FACTS

THE TANK BULLDOZER, OR TERRIER:

- weighs 32 tons (29 mt), is 19.7 feet (6 m) long and 8.2 feet (2.5 m) wide
- has a top speed of 44.7 mph (72 km/h)
- uses five onboard cameras to get 360-degree views night and day, whatever the conditions
- can be operated by what looks like a video game console about 0.4 miles (0.6 km) away!

WHAT ELSE CAN THE TERRIER DO?

With its various attachments, the Terrier can dig holes, drill concrete, lift objects, clear minefields and, thanks to its caterpillar tracks, cross ditches up to 6.6 feet (2 m) wide. When operators are inside its cab they can defend themselves with the Terrier's machine gun and smoke grenades.

WHAT'S THE POINT OF THE TERRIER?

The tank gives protection to the troops who use it. Its remote control means, in certain dangerous situations, its operators can keep a safe distance.

Didn't you know?
The Terrier can move up to 298 tons (270 mt) of earth in an hour – that's about the volume of two double-decker buses!

THE FACTS

THE MERCEDES FUTURE TRUCK 2025:

- drives itself automatically, and knows when a vehicle is overtaking because of its outside motion sensors
- is powered by a 12.8-liter, 6-cylinder diesel engine
- can see up to 330 feet (100 m) ahead, thanks to a 3-D camera that detects cars, pedestrians, objects in the road, road markings and traffic signs
- can connect to the Internet to communicate with other vehicles

WHAT ELSE CAN THE TRUCK DO?

The Future Truck can maintain a steady speed on boring highway journeys, keeping fuel consumption low, and freeing drivers to do other work. They have to stay awake though, or the truck will slow down and pull over.

WHAT'S THE POINT OF BEING DRIVERLESS?

Around the world, an average of 3,400 people die on the roads each day. Most accidents are caused by human error. Computers don't get tired, so the driverless truck won't lose concentration.

Didn't you know?
The inspiration for the look of the Future Truck came from outfits worn by French pop band, Daft Punk.

AND FINALLY ...

While 60 Terriers are already at work with the British Army, the Future Truck is just that – a truck of the future. The technology is available though, and could make 24-hour deliveries more efficient. However, laws need to change before we will see driverless vehicles on the roads.

WE CHOSE

The Terrier – but grab that console and stand well back!

TRAVEL FROM LONDON TO PARIS BY EUROSTAR TRAIN . . . OR FLYING CAR?

Eighteen Eurostar trains travel between London and Paris each day, covering the 213.6 miles (343.9 km) in 2 hours 15 minutes. The larger trains are just under half a kilometer long, and can carry up to 770 passengers. Just over 31 miles (50 km) of the journey is via the Channel Tunnel, 164 to 246 feet (50–75 m) below the sea!

Drive your Aeromobil to the nearest airfield, press a button to open out the wings, adjust the gears to power the propeller and switch to flying controls. With a top speed of 124 miles per hour (200 km/h) and a distance of 430 miles (692 km), the Aeromobil could make it to Paris in under two hours, using far less fuel than a car when it's gliding.

Didn't you know?
The Aeromobil is small enough to slot into a single parking space.

AND FINALLY ...

You can land the Aeromobil in a farmer's field, but it will need a clear 164 feet (50 m), and 656 feet (200 m) for takeoff – that's hard to find in the city center. Step straight from the Eurostar in London or Paris, and you're quickly connected with public transport.

WE CHOSE

Eurostar. Glide into the city on a set of rails.

3-D PRINT YOUR OWN HOUSE ... OR CAR?

Building began on the world's first 3-D printed house in Amsterdam at the beginning of 2014. It needed a specially built 3-D printer that's 20 feet (6 m) tall to make plastic parts that will become the walls of this futuristic structure. The plan is to recycle plastic waste to make new homes in overcrowded cities around the world.

The first ever 3-D printed car was also designed and made in 2014 from 49 printed body parts – instead of the usual 5,000! The tires, wheels, electric battery, suspension and windshield were made in the usual way, but the body, chassis and dashboard were printed from black plastic, reinforced with carbon fiber. It all took just 44 hours.

WE CHOSE

The car – for now. While the house is just a prototype, which will hopefully be used around the world one day, the car actually works.

RIDE A TRAIN THAT FLOATS ABOVE THE TRACKS ... OR A BOAT THAT FLOATS OVER WATER?

THE FACTS

THE MAGLEV TRAIN:

- **doesn't have wheels**
- **doesn't have an engine, so it doesn't give off harmful emissions**
- **doesn't really have a proper driver**

THE FACTS

A HOVERCRAFT:

- **floats on a cushion of air**
- **is amphibious: it can come out of the water to land on any flattish surface**
- **uses half as much fuel as a same-sized boat and can travel twice as fast**

HOW DOES A MAGLEV MOVE?

Maglev is short for magnetic levitation. Using electromagnetic pull, these trains can float above their tracks, or guideways. Waves of magnetic energy produced by generators in the guideways move the train along.

WHERE CAN I RIDE A MAGLEV?

Shanghai's maglev trains are the fastest passenger trains in the world, running 18.6 miles (30 km) from the city center to the airport, with a top speed of 268 miles per hour (431 km/h). Japan's new maglevs won't operate until 2027, but they're expected to make the 200-mile (322-km) journey between Tokyo and Nagoya in just 40 minutes!

SO HOW DOES A HOVERCRAFT MOVE?

A fan forces air into the inflatable rubber cushion underneath the craft and it rises up. The engine creates thrust, to make the craft move forward and the "pilot" steers the rudder to change direction. The craft floats on air rather than water, so there's no friction between the boat and the water. That's why it can move so fast.

WHERE CAN I RIDE A HOVERCRAFT?

Hovercraft are best used in hard-to-reach areas, such as shallow or icy waters, or mudflats. They're popular with the military, but some people race smaller hovercraft for fun!

Didn't you know?
Experiments with a hair dryer, one can inside another and some weighing scales helped the hovercraft inventor develop his idea in the 1950s.

AND FINALLY ...

Traveling at 62 miles per hour (100 km/h) in a hovercraft can be a bumpy experience, but on a maglev train, even at 249 miles per hour (400 km/h), you won't feel the speed.

WE CHOSE

The maglev. One day maglev technology might even be used to launch vehicles into space, reducing the huge cost of fuel used on takeoff.

LOOK COOL IN A CLASSIC VW BEETLE … OR A FIAT 500?

The first Volkswagen Beetle was designed by Ferdinand Porsche in 1937 especially for families (bottom left). It was a four-seater, with an air-cooled engine (at the back!), that was cheap to run. The original Beetle proved to be very reliable, and kept on selling until 2003!

The first Fiat 500 was designed by Dante Giacosa in 1957 as Italy's family car (bottom right). Like the Beetle, its air-cooled engine was at the back – the doors opened backwards too. At only 10 feet (3 m) long, it was designed to be affordable – the stylish sunroof that stretched the length of the roof was actually a way to use less steel!

AND FINALLY …

The Beetle was designed on the orders of Adolf Hitler – definitely not cool! At its launch in 1957, a parade of 500s drove through the streets of Turin, each with a fashion model standing in the back, to a reception from the King of Belgium, a future Pope and other Italian celebrities. Now that was super-cool!

WE CHOSE

The Fiat 500.

Didn't you know?
The Beetle was so well finished it was practically watertight and could float for a few minutes on water!

WHAT WOULD YOU CHOOSE?

AN E-BIKE ... OR SEGWAY TO RIDE INTO TOWN?

An e-bike looks like an ordinary bike, with an added motor and rechargeable battery. A sensor tells the motor how much help you need with pedaling and, once power assisted, you'll fly uphill! The e-bike's electric engine can't drive the bike faster than 15 miles per hour (24 km/h) – but you can!

On a Segway you stand between two wheels, and simply lean forward to speed up, backwards to slow down (there are no brakes!) and left or right to steer. The Segway does your balancing for you, using gyroscopes and a built-in computer, and has a top speed of around 12 miles per hour (20 km/h).

Didn't you know?
You don't "ride" on a Segway, you "glide."

WE CHOSE

The e-bike. In some countries, you can only use a Segway on private roads. However, the European Union has now officially agreed that e-bikes are a healthy, emission-free answer to city center traffic trouble.

TAKE A BUS FUELED BY POOP ... OR A SOLAR CAR CALLED STELLA?

Didn't you know?
The side of the biobus is decorated with pictures of people sitting on the toilet!

THE FACTS

THE BIOBUS:

- first hit the road in Bath, Somerset, UK, in 2014
- is powered by a renewable and sustainable fuel (human poop and food waste), producing fewer emissions than diesel
- can carry up to 40 people and travel up to 186 miles (300 km) without needing to refuel

HOW MUCH POOP DOES THE BUS NEED?

It takes a year's supply of poop from five people to fill the tank just once! The supply isn't likely to run out, however, because Bristol sewage works processes 2.6 billion cubic feet (75 million m^3) of sewage waste and 35,500 tons (32.205 mt) of food waste each year!

DOESN'T THE BUS SMELL?

No. Bacteria in the anaerobic digester break down all biodegradable material in the waste to produce biomethane gas, which powers the bus. The impurities are extracted, so the fuel hardly smells at all.

WHAT MAKES STELLA SO GREAT?

Solar panels convert the Sun's rays into electricity and charge Stella's lithium battery. Stella is the first "energy positive" car (she creates more energy than she uses). The excess energy can charge up other gadgets. She's built from aluminum and carbon fiber and weighs just 838 pounds (380 kg).

HOW FAR CAN SHE GO?

Stella can travel up to 550 miles (885 km) when fully charged, and drive in daylight further than any of today's electric cars. In 2013, Stella won the Cruiser Class in the World Solar Challenge, racing 1,864 miles (3,000 km) from Darwin to Adelaide, Australia, against other solar cars. She averaged 37 miles per hour (60 km/h), with a top speed of 74.5 miles per hour (120 km/h).

THE FACTS

STELLA, THE SOLAR-POWERED CAR:

- **was developed by a team of Dutch technology students**
- **is fueled by solar panels on her roof**
- **can comfortably carry a family of four with their luggage and travel up to 550 miles (885 km) on one charge**
- **is 15 feet (4.6 m) long, but only 4 feet (1.2 m) tall**

AND FINALLY . . .

Stella is licensed to go on the road, but she's the only one of her kind so far. Biobuses don't just exist in Bristol, they're used in other parts of the UK and Sweden too.

WE CHOSE

Public transport wins at the moment, so take the poop-bus, but keep your eyes peeled for more solar-powered cars.

RACE THE PORSCHE P2 SEMPER VIVUS HYBRID ... OR THE FERRARI 125S?

WE CHOSE

The Ferrari – it's the first in a long line of dream cars. Produced in 1900, the P2 (above, left) was the second car made by Porsche and the first hybrid car EVER. The P2 reached 20 miles per hour (32 km/h), and could cover 37 miles (60 km) when fully charged. The first Ferrari EVER, the 125S, was produced 47 years later (above, right). It was designed for speed, and could hit 106 miles per hour (170 km/h) and go from 0 to 62 miles per hour (100 km/h) in 10.8 seconds.

TRACK YOUR FITNESS WITH YOUR SMART WATCH ... OR YOUR SMART SHIRT?

WE CHOSE

The shirt. Covering a greater surface area, the smart shirt can keep a larger number of microsensors close to your skin, measuring your speed, location and heart rate. It sends the information via a transmitter to a smartphone. Some fabrics can even be recharged when they're washed and ironed!

Didn't you know?
Your shoes can tell you where to go! Connect a pair of "Haptic" shoes to a smartphone, and they'll vibrate to tell you whether to turn left or right.

WHAT WOULD YOU CHOOSE?

TAKE A TOUR ON A HIPPO BUS THAT FLOATS ... OR A CAMEL BUS WITH HUMPS?

Havana, Cuba's camel bus (above) has one cab, two humps and eighteen wheels. Old buses welded unevenly together create the hump effect, while a tractor cab pulls the bus along – with up to 300 commuting passengers inside!

Take a Hippo bus-boat tour in Victoria, Canada (below), and your bus will leave the road and plunge – like a hippo – into the Pacific Ocean! This converted school bus follows the style of military amphibious landing craft, rolling along roads and floating in water.

WE CHOSE

The Hippo. With no air conditioning, Cubans were relieved when the camel buses started going out of service. The Hippo buses are carefully tested, so that their 40 passengers are safe on board to have fun and stay dry (the bus is completely waterproof).

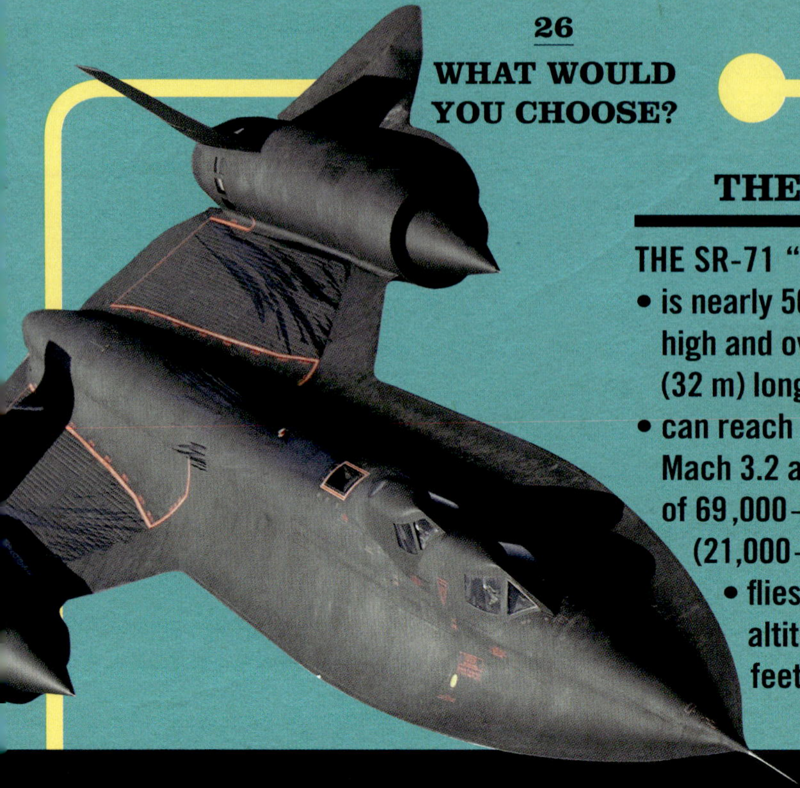

THE FACTS

THE SR-71 "BLACKBIRD":

- is nearly 56 feet (17 m) high and over 105 feet (32 m) long
- can reach speeds over Mach 3.2 at an altitude of 69,000–85,300 feet (21,000–26,000 m)
- flies at a maximum altitude of 450,000 feet (137,000 m)

BREAK THE SOUND BARRIER IN A LAND ROCKET ... OR A PLANE THAT FLIES LIKE A ROCKET?

WHAT'S IT LIKE TO FLY A BLACKBIRD?

More like a spaceship than an aircraft, you'll need to wear a pressure suit to survive the altitude. The engine accelerates so fast that within two minutes of lift-off you're at 24,000 feet (7,315 m)!

WHAT'S SPECIAL ABOUT THE WAY THE PLANE IS MADE?

After breaking the sound barrier, the temperature soars to over 644° F (340° C), but the plane's lightweight titanium body is built to cope with the heat. The Blackbird gets its name from its special black paint that can absorb radar signals. To radar equipment on the ground the plane looks smaller than a person!

WHAT WOULD YOU CHOOSE?

WHAT'S IT LIKE TO DRIVE A ROCKET CAR?

At first you'll feel like you're in a plane speeding up for takeoff, but you'll just keep rolling. Up to 298 miles per hour (480 km/h) can feel quite bumpy, then approaching the speed of sound, 768 miles per hour (1,236 km/h – Mach 1), a shock wave is created and your clear view becomes misty. The noise is incredible!

WHAT'S SPECIAL ABOUT THE BLOODHOUND?

The cockpit is made from a single piece of carbon fiber and took 10,000 hours to design and build. The roof is shaped to slow airflow to the engines at the back. The solid aluminum wheels have to stay on the ground.

THE FACTS

THE BLOODHOUND SSC:

- **is around 46 feet (14 m) long and weighs 8.3 tons (7.5 mt)**
- **is called a supersonic car (SSC), because it's designed to travel faster than the speed of sound**
- **looks like a rocket, but is classed as a car because it has four wheels and is controlled by a driver**

AND FINALLY ...

Andy Green's 1997 land speed record of 763 miles per hour (1,228 km/h) still stands. No one else has ever broken the sound barrier on land. The Blackbird has flown at over three times the speed of sound, 2,175 miles per hour (3,500 km/h – Mach 3.2) over 1,000 times.

WE CHOSE

The Blackbird. It's not in service anymore, but it's still the fastest manned jet plane in the world.

Didn't you know?

The Bloodhound SSC is powered by a jet engine and Formula One engines. They produce 135,000 horsepower – the equivalent of 180 Formula One cars!

GET RESCUED BY A TIGER ... OR A PUMA?

WE CHOSE

The Puma. Both helicopters are made by the same company and fitted with automatic flight control systems and automatic hovering. However, while the Super Puma (left) can be equipped for search and rescue missions – with rescue seats, stretchers and a hoist – the Tiger (above) is designed for attack! It comes with antitank missiles and a turreted gun that can fire 750 rounds per minute.

CAPTAIN A GIANT CARGO SHIP ... OR A JUMBO CATAMARAN?

WE CHOSE

The catamaran. Named the Pieter Schelte, *it's actually the biggest ship in the world, measuring 1,253 feet (382 m) long and 406 feet (124 m) wide. The largest cargo ships operate computerized cranes to load up to 18,000 color-coded containers. The twin-hull catamaran shape enables the* Pieter Schelte *to raise 73,000 tons (66,000 mt) of oil rig – in two parts – and take it to a new location.*

WHAT WOULD YOU CHOOSE?

OBSERVE EARTH FROM ONE HUGE SATELLITE ... OR FROM LOTS OF LITTLE ONES THE SIZE OF A BIRD?

Landsats (below, right) are designed and built by NASA. They've been orbiting and scanning Earth since the 1970s, relaying images showing Earth's changing land and resource use. Large satellites like these can be the size of a small house, weigh over 6,600 pounds (3,000 kg) and take up to ten years to build! A mini satellite, called the "Dove" (above), was designed in a garage. It's the size of a shoe box, weighs 11 pounds (5 kg), and has a telescope. Creators of the Dove plan to have 100 of them orbiting Earth at once, to keep track of changes in forestry, fishing, agriculture and climate.

AND FINALLY ...

The Landsat costs millions of dollars to build, while the Dove is cheap to make. Landsat 8 scans the whole Earth every 16 days, but the Dove will do this every day.

WE CHOSE

The Dove. Why have one satellite when you can have 100?

Didn't you know?
Disused satellites make up some of the 13,000 items of human-made space junk orbiting our planet that will eventually fall back to Earth.

30
WHAT WOULD YOU CHOOSE?

GO TO THE BEACH IN A 1970S VW CAMPER WITH A POP-TOP ROOF ... OR AN ELEMMENT PALAZZO MOTOR HOME WITH A POP-UP ROOF TERRACE?

WE CHOSE

The VW Camper. The Elemment Palazzo is 39 feet (12 m) long, and may have a fridge, dishwasher, and an upstairs with a bedroom, bathroom and roof terrace (which pops up at the push of a button), but it comes with a $2.6 million price tag. Simply push up the VW Camper pop-top roof by hand and – ta-da – you'll find two bunk beds! Who needs a roof terrace?

MEET A ROBOT THAT CAN READ YOUR EMOTIONS ... OR ONE THAT SHOWS EMOTION?

WE CHOSE

The emotion-reading robot called Pepper. The Japanese karakuri robot operates through a clockwork mechanism and shows emotion after he shoots his arrow and it misses. His face seems disappointed! This is 200-year-old technology, though, and the emotion is only a clever illusion. Pepper, however, is a cutting-edge Japanese robot that uses artificial intelligence to read your emotions when he talks to you.

GLOSSARY

2-stroke engine – An engine that completes a power cycle with two strokes (two up-and-down movements) of the piston, rather than four (which happens in a 4-stroke engine).

altitude – Height above the surface of the Earth.

anaerobic digester – A large container where tiny organisms break down organic matter (without oxygen).

artificial intelligence – A computer system developed to perform tasks normally requiring human intelligence, such as decision-making.

carbon emissions – Carbon dioxide that is released by vehicles such as cars, planes and buses when they are fueled by gasoline or diesel.

electromagnetic – The use of magnetic fields (of attraction and repulsion) to suspend one object above another.

exoskeleton – The name for the external skeleton around an insect that supports and protects its body. A powered exoskeleton is worn by a person and boosts their strength or endurance.

friction – Resistance generated when one surface rubs against another.

gear – A metal wheel with "teeth" that works with other toothed wheels to change the speed of a vehicle or engine.

gyroscope – A device consisting of a wheel or a disc mounted so that it can spin freely around an axis.

hybrid – Refers to a vehicle powered by an electric motor and a conventional engine.

Mach – An unusually high speed – the ratio of the speed of an object compared to the speed of sound.

pneumatic – Containing air or using air pressure to make something move or work.

public transport – Trains, buses, underground trains and other forms of transport that everyone can use if they buy a ticket.

renewable energy – A natural source of energy that will not run out, such as wind power, solar power or wave power.

solar cells/solar panel – A device that can convert the power of the Sun into electricity.

sound barrier – The increased drag and other forces that act on an object that is approaching the speed of sound.

sustainable – An action that avoids using up resources.

WEBSITES

www.bbc.com/future/tags/sustainability
Collection of BBC articles relating to sustainability and the future of science and technology.

http://science.howstuffworks.com/mega-machines-videos-playlist.htm
Videos explaining the work of various megamachines.

INDEX